Navigating a Teacher's First Year

A Guidebook for Districts, Administrators and Instructional Coaches

CINDY DANIELS AND KAREN MARTIN

Navigating A Teacher's First Year: A Guidebook for Districts, Administrators, and Instructional Coaches

by Cindy Daniels and Karen Martin

Published by Perfect Bound Marketing +Press
www.perfectboundmarketing.press
Peoria, Arizona

Print ISBN: 978-1-939614-96-4

e-book ISBN: 978-1-939614-97-1

Cover illustrated by Raquel Omana

TABLE OF CONTENTS

Foreword _____iii

Introduction _____vi

Starting The Engine—First Thoughts _____viii

Chapter 1 –Being Ready When the Students Arrive
*Preparing For the Destination*_____1

Chapter 2 –Adjusting as the Year Begins
Ready for Takeoff! _____9

Chapter 3 –Educational Overload of Information and
Deadlines *Buckle Up!* _____18

Chapter 4 –Implementing Lessons and Assessments
Attaining Results in the First Semester _____24

Chapter 5 –Curriculum Goals And Instruction
Exploring the Landscape! _____29

Chapter 6 –Observing The Students' Learning Patterns
Watching The Signs and Checking The Map _____33

Chapter 7 –Have the Learning Indicators Been Achieved?
How to End the Year and Reach the Destination _____37

Chapter 8 –Thinking Ahead—Reflection
Adjusting The Mirrors _____41

Chapter 9 –Mentoring Other Staff Members
Shifting All the Gears _____44

Chapter 10 –Charging the Battery
Using the Resources _____47

Keep the Engine Running—Final Thoughts _____60

Acknowledgments _____61

Take the Next Step _____62

FOREWORD

"I think the teaching profession contributes more to the future of our society than any other single profession."

−John Wooden

"The delicate balance of mentoring someone is not creating them in your own image, but giving them the opportunity to create themselves."

−Steven Spielberg

New teachers come to the profession with tremendous enthusiasm. They truly believe they are ready for any challenge. In most instances, however, they are not prepared for the rigors of actually teaching a classroom of students and the many challenges that come from a multitude of directions. As a former mentor and director of professional development who worked closely with outstanding mentors such as Cindy Daniels and Karen Martin, I can attest to the importance of a highly trained and skillful mentor in counseling and supporting a budding teacher.

In this day and age, districts cannot afford to lose teachers. Beyond the investment in recruiting and hiring, there is a severe teacher shortage. If teachers experience success in their first few years, they are more likely to stay in the profession. We all have heard that job-embedded professional development is the best form of professional learning, and there is no better job-embedded professional development than learning from a master practitioner.

That being said, it is unfortunate that many school districts cannot afford a full-time mentor whose only responsibility is to support and nurture novice teachers. Gone are the days where new teachers just "sink or swim." As mentioned, districts can no longer afford that, not to mention that students in the "sinking" rooms will never get that year back and the academic repercussions may have lasting effects. Every school district and administrator must do everything in their power to ensure there is a "safety net" for all students. One way of doing so is to provide a detailed guide for success—a guide that administrators and colleagues can turn to—to assist beginning teachers. Everyone is then on the same page, and the new teacher can review lists of needs and/or procedures. Once the basics are covered, they can focus on the actual "art" of teaching.

Beginning teachers often "don't know what they don't know." They often don't even know which questions to ask. This process eliminates the confusion. Identifying those needs and procedures for a safe and productive learning environment will certainly set the stage for a novice teacher and provide a nice foundation from which they can build.

–Julie Salley, Director of Professional Development, Paradise Valley Unified School District, Retired

Regardless of profession, a good mentor often means the difference between success and failure. An effective mentor is more than a coach or counselor and realizes that each individual has specific strengths and needs. While it may seem obvious that a young, new teacher right out of college would need a mentor, it is also critically important for anyone entering the field of education to have someone they trust to give them honest feedback and direction. I began my career as a teacher after 20 years in the business world. I had different needs than those beginning their first careers. Karen Martin realized that I may not need help in some areas already honed by my business career, but I needed assistance in other areas.

Karen and Cindy have decades of combined teaching experience and have seen the good, the bad, and the ugly! They understand the individual needs of teachers and address the commonalities of great teaching. Teaching is art and science, and Karen and Cindy celebrate the unique strengths of individual teachers while guiding each teacher through the hurdles that become insurmountable to many. I have the greatest job in the world, but I can honestly say I wouldn't be here if not for the mentoring I received from these two talented, genuine professionals.

–Dr. Yvonne M. Perot, AP Psychology, Horizon High School, Paradise Valley Unified School District

INTRODUCTION

This book is written for those professionals whose role it is to enter the world of a first-year teacher, have a heightened awareness of the minute details that await a promising professional, and guide novice teachers to a productive and fulfilling first year with their students. It is specifically written to provide administrators with information about the nuts-and-bolts needs of a new teacher/staff member and to provide organized checklists of ways to support them. The combined 80-plus years of experience in K–12 education that Cindy Daniels and Karen Martin bring to this book encompass the roles of teacher, specialist, mentor, professional development presenter, supervisor, and administrator.

An educational dilemma that faces our schools in the 21st century is the lack of qualified teachers; the following statistics provide a glimpse into that reality:

- States spend $1–2.2 billion a year on teacher turnover when they could be investing in a strong induction process for a fraction of the cost. (Alliance)

- "A high quality induction program not only produces student achievement, but also reduces teacher turnover and yields a 66% increase in retention of teachers after five years. Research also states that the most effective component in student achievement is the teacher in the classroom." NTC

- Teacher quality has more impact on student achievement than any other school-based factor. (Harvard)

- "Students taught by an effective teacher score 50% higher than those students taught by an ineffective teacher." Linda Darling-Hammond, The Brookings Institute

This book is a chronological map of how to prepare for and thrive in an academic year, including organization, communication, lesson design, classroom climate, assessment, and more. It is not another book on learning to coach and mentor, but rather a book to guide administrators, principals, and instructional coaches in their day-to-day interaction with novice teachers. Chapter 10 includes 86 resources to further support the novice teacher on the topics addressed in each chapter. They are organized by chapter for easy reference.

This book is not intended to replace a formal new-teacher induction program, but rather to complement what may already be in place for new teachers in any district or corporation. The questions, ideas, and relevant information presented need to be considered, examined, and answered through the lens of individual districts, school beliefs, values, missions, and curricula. Along our journey, many administrators have requested this type of resource to better support their instructional coaches and novice teachers when mentors are not part of their staffing. Thus, this book can be used in conjunction with an existing program or can be the fundamental resource for supporting new teachers.

Teachers learn best in collaborative environment, not in isolation. They thrive when supported. Teachers want to have strong bonds and a common vision to move student academics forward. Educators have been discussing this need since the early 1990s; it is time to navigate this journey for all who are entering the teaching profession so that the teacher shortage can be minimized. Our children deserve qualified effective teachers in their classrooms; this book delivers the essentials to make that happen.

STARTING THE IGNITION— FIRST THOUGHTS

Teaching is the only profession where 99 percent competency is expected on the first day of the job. While teachers support each other as best they can, there are not enough hours in the day for a veteran teacher to do his/her own job and also be available to answer a new educator's daily questions. A few minutes at lunch, during prep time, or even before or after school now and then do not provide the consistent support that a novice teacher requires. Since not all teachers—even master teachers—are specifically trained in the skill of mentoring, they cannot be expected to provide the comprehensive work that is necessary to steer novice educators in the direction of excellence.

This book addresses ideas to consider when welcoming any and all new staff members to a school. When each new member of the school community has clear and common expectations and is confident in his/her role, the school can operate efficiently and prioritize the students' safety and achievement. A Harvard University study noted that "Teacher quality has more impact on student achievement than any other school-based factor."

Less than half of employees are excited about their jobs.

–Harvey Mackay

Investing time in training from the beginning will convey to novice teachers that your school values both teachers and students. Building confidence in new teachers will result in their participation and engagement in the school community. Expediting the process will allow novice teachers to feel a part of the whole picture and lead to job satisfaction.

Supporting new teachers looks like:

- Information being provided
- A "go-to" person being clearly established and communicated with
- Your presence via brief meetings, walk-throughs, etc.
- A welcoming staff to new colleagues
- A respectful staff that acknowledges what new colleagues bring to the table
- A helpful staff that will lend a hand
- Professional development opportunities being provided to help new teachers develop the habit of lifelong learning

Supporting new teachers sounds like:

- Feedback provided that is not evaluative
- Concerns being listened to and often without comment
- Probing questions being asked to help the new teacher find his/her own voice and solutions
- Concrete solutions being explored, provided, and executed

CHAPTER 1

Being Ready
When the Students Arrive

Preparing for the Destination

*"If you don't know where you are going,
you'll end up somewhere else."*

–Yogi Berra

EXPERIENCE TELLS US

"Student learning suffers when inexperienced teachers struggle alone to meet their wide-ranging needs or lose precious class time establishing and maintaining structures that keep students engaged in productive learning."

–Ellen Moir, featured blog: Change the Odds by Strengthening New Teacher Induction, October 21, 2016

There are myriad school-specific procedures to consider when preparing for the journey of a school year. Addressing the expectations with all stakeholders and how they will contribute to your school will enhance the overall learning climate. The practices related to hall passes, restroom usage, nurse visits, etc. need to be clearly communicated. Opening the school year is second nature to you and your current staff, but not to new teachers who will want to be informed, competent, and involved.

Data tells us that new teachers who are mentored stay in the profession longer than the typical three years that many non-mentored teachers spend before leaving due to lack of support (Carnegie Foundation for the Advancement of Teaching, 2015). Effective teaching leads to increased student achievement: "When new teachers also had strong support from school administrators and other teachers, they were three to four times more likely to want to remain in their school. Importantly, these teachers also moved the needle for student achievement" (Stanford Research Institute/SRI International Evaluation, 2016).

It is imperative that someone is assigned the privilege of providing support to the new teachers on your faculty. The urgency of this support cannot be emphasized enough; it must be implemented and **sustained** in a deliberate and organized manner throughout every novice teacher's first year.

Benjamin Franklin, Fred Jones, and years of experience have told us: "If you fail to plan, you are planning to fail!" New teachers must be cognizant of the host of preparations that must be handled even before their students arrive. This foundation is paramount to the success of the school year. Intentional and purposeful preparation will result in a solid start to their year. To best prepare new teachers, it is incumbent on the administration to have systems in place when new teachers arrive. No matter what time of year they arrive, this process should accommodate their needs.

> *When new teachers also had strong support from school administrators and other teachers, they were three to four times more likely to want to remain in their school. Importantly, these teachers also moved the needle for student achievement.*
>
> –Stanford Research Institute

BEST PRACTICES ... FOR SETTING UP A SAFE AND FUNCTIONAL LEARNING ENVIRONMENT

New teachers expect and deserve the support of their administration and colleagues. This can be demonstrated by affirming their skills and welcoming them as the school's "new blood." In addition to the items outlined in this chapter, new teachers need to know the district landscape. Information about paychecks, insurance, personal and sick days, technology, and district new-teacher policies can cause unnecessary stress unless there is a method for relaying it. New teachers should be made aware of how to access this critical information.

Whose responsibility is it to have the basic classroom equipment prepared for new teachers? Providing a shoulder partner/neighbor teacher/colleague/plant manager to help them weave their way through preparing their classroom and getting needed equipment, their ID, and their keys/fobs is critical, as these issues cause much anxiety before the school year begins. Wherever this responsibility lies, it needs to happen. New teachers will depend on you to have these procedures in place. If you don't, you are setting up your new staff members for failure. An inventory list in each classroom is highly recommended for keeping classrooms stocked and complete from year to year. New teachers need your support in creating a space where students can thrive.

Below are components that should be present and functioning in a classroom assigned to a new teacher:

- teacher desk
- teacher chair
- teacher stool/high chair
- student desks/tables
- student chairs
- storage closet(s)

- pencil sharpener(s)
- shelves
- U.S. flag
- tables
- lights
- media cart
- LCD projector
- smartboard
- file cabinets
- screen
- whiteboards
- bulletin boards
- clean and repaired carpet/tile

Instructional Materials

- laptops/iPads
- textbooks
- workbooks
- dictionaries
- supplemental materials

As new teachers begin to set up their own classrooms, the following are also items to consider:

- **Classroom**
  - Provisions need to be in place for unneeded and unwanted classroom materials/furniture left from previous teachers.
  - Suggest that the new teachers absorb their space and think about the traffic pattern of students and how their seating arrangement will best accommodate effective teaching strategies.

- Along with the seating arrangement, they should consider the room layout and other furniture and materials. New teachers should also be encouraged to change their seating arrangement and room layout if they find that what they are currently using is not effective for them or their students.

- Each teacher should also check lights, ceiling tiles, carpet squares, chairs, and desks for inadequacies that might need custodial/maintenance support.

- Have new teachers make a list of their specific needs, such as podium, high stool, or file cabinet(s), and inform them how to make this request, both for the beginning of the year and during the school year. Alert your custodial staff to be attentive to the needs of new teachers for this process.

- Let teachers know that it's okay to be concerned and ask questions about their classroom.

The following is additional information for a teacher's classroom:

- Can items such as tissues, bandages, hand sanitizer, etc., be requested as a donation from parents? Do teachers need to provide these items themselves?

- What is provided by their grade level/department/school/district budget? Who provides their budget line for ordering materials?

- What else may they need to procure for their own classroom?

- **Curriculum, Online Resources, Other Resources**

  The questions below are not intended to overwhelm school leaders who support new teachers; they are simply food for thought on addressing the many needs that may be overlooked.

- How and when are new teachers trained for the online grading system and other essential online programs used at your school?

- What are the procedures for obtaining and distributing books to the students?

- Where do new teachers get their Teacher's Edition materials, planning books, and grade book information?

- What expendable supplies are available to new teachers?

- What, if any, budget does the team, department, or individual have?

- How do new teachers acquire their computers and other related technology equipment?

- Where do new teachers obtain their daily schedules?

- Where do new teachers go to obtain the class roster(s)? How do they know if they have any special needs students or students who require accommodations such as seating, lighting, or hearing?

- **Classroom Management—Paving a Pathway for a Positive Learning Environment**

  - Lesson design is key in managing student behavior. Student engagement, learner variability, pacing, being prepared, over planning, and teaching the standards are integral to a well-designed lesson. Using a variety of strategies reaches many types and levels of learners in every classroom. New teachers will need guidance to learn how to effectively execute a solid lesson plan.

  - Motivation may seem like a vague piece of the classroom management picture. There are, in fact, very deliberate ways you can help new teachers motivate their students. A few suggestions include:

- ◆ Authentic praise for students' work, progress, and behavior
- ◆ High expectations followed by accountability for achieving those expectations
- ◆ Timely and specific feedback to student work
- ◆ Enthusiasm for their subject matter
- ◆ Connection with their students' world
- ◆ Attendance at their students' performances and competitions

- ▪ Managing student behavior need not be a daunting endeavor when lesson design and motivation are skillfully implemented. Using a calm instructional voice, moving throughout the classroom, practicing routines and procedures, and having a plan for respectfully handling situations that arise in the classroom are all subtle techniques for managing a classroom full of students. Some new teachers will be adept in this domain; most will find classroom management one of the most difficult challenges of their first year of teaching. Make your new teachers aware of any schoolwide programs that are in place, and guide them through the process.

Refer to Chapter 10 for additional resources for classroom organization, preparation, and management.

ROADBLOCKS AND DETOURS

Lack of communication with district office personnel, school administration, designated staff, and new teachers can cause confusion and disorganization for the new teacher. Availability of assigned staff to mentor novice teachers is paramount to making new teachers feel welcomed and to having productive days before school begins.

Communicate your support for your new teachers with a strong message: "We acknowledge that you are a new teacher at our school, and we have a system in place to assist you and accommodate your needs. We want you to be prepared for your students so that you can execute your job as a teaching professional from day one." Lack of follow-through will hinder new teachers from being completely prepared and ready for the students. The quality of preparation will ultimately impact student achievement as well as teacher satisfaction and retention.

–Ellen Moir, Featured Blog: New Teacher Center, October 31, 2016

"Student learning suffers when inexperienced teachers struggle alone to meet their wide-ranging needs or lose precious class time establishing and maintaining structures that keep students engaged and productively learning. In the face of these challenges, many new teachers feel that they aren't supported when they take charge of their first classroom. Few new teachers possess the skills they need to provide the best education to children across all circumstances straight out of their preparation program. Even the most promising new teachers need help to accelerate their development and learn how to really make a difference for children of diverse skill levels and backgrounds."

CHAPTER 2

Adjusting as the Year Begins

Ready for Takeoff!

*"A teacher affects eternity; he can never tell
where his influence stops."*

–Henry Adams

EXPERIENCE TELLS US

In teaching, a novice professional is expected to perform the same duties at the same level as veteran educators on day one and every day after that. This is one of the only professions in which proficiency is expected immediately. Providing support for new teachers in the initial weeks of the school year is crucial for both the teachers' confidence and the students' achievement throughout the entire academic year. Since expectations for the novice are equal to those for the veteran, continued specific and purposeful support is paramount to success. In addition to your informational support, new teachers can benefit from your feedback. Feedback can be as simple as a thumbs-up after observing a few minutes of a lesson, a brief note on the desk, a congratulatory comment in the hallway, or a confidence-boosting email. Novice teachers want and expect an instructional leader to help move their practice forward with reflective feedback on their daily performances of delivering instruction and engaging students. Getting in their classrooms often during the first quarter—even for five minutes at a time—will allow you to observe new teachers' performance. It will also provide you with substantive information to determine whether intervention strategies are needed as well as an opportunity to affirm your new teachers' strengths and contributions to your school. Anecdotal research-based data, as addressed in Chapter One, continues to indicate that making mentoring and guiding new teachers priorities for your school will improve retention rates, student achievement, and school climate.

BEST PRACTICES ... FOR PROCEDURE PREPARING

Experienced teachers have productive routines that have become habit due to years of development, repetition, and fine tuning. Novice educators might find the sheer number of daily routine requirements overwhelming during the first few weeks if they are not addressed properly. These routines and procedures must be clearly written and shared with new teachers, either in a binder or digitally. New teachers also need to know how to access information about the school's routines—and that they are responsible for it. They need to know that they are expected to read the school manual(s), discipline procedures, and any other specific information for their school and be responsible for the content.

Novice educators might find the sheer number of daily routine requirements overwhelming during the first few weeks if they are not addressed properly.

The following are essential points of information to orient new teachers to your procedures and expectations:

- **Arrival for all Levels**
  - Entering the classroom (pre-K–6) (7–8) (9–12). All grade levels have different expectations for this procedure.

- The importance of taking attendance as a state regulation must be communicated.

- Explain the process for students who are tardy.

- **Recess**

  - PreK-3 students will need to be taught how to play and what the school's specific expectations are for the playground, such as not picking up or throwing rocks, using the playground equipment, sharing the use of swings, the proper way to go down the slide, etc.

  - Consider what games are not allowed at your school.

  - Grades 4–6 will need reminding of expectations to eliminate the "I forgot" or "being new to the school" proverbial excuses.

- **Cafeteria**

  - K–3 grade-procedures of how students get through the line, how they obtain their ticket, lunch number, etc., can be quite overwhelming for the first few weeks for the teacher as well as the students.

  - Where do they sit? How do they sit? How to get help from an aide? Which restrooms to use if needed? How does their food get thrown away, and what happens when they are done eating? Where do they go next? These are many of the procedures that need to be clearly communicated to the teacher and practiced by the students.

  - How does the school post, teach, and follow through with expectations for students to behave in the cafeteria? This is a million-dollar question, as setting expectations for your class is important. How they treat each other, the volume level with which they speak to each other, eating, and cleaning up are important parts of cafeteria behavior.

- **Dismissal for Pre-K–6**

  - Each grade level has different expectations for this procedure.

  - Communicate the importance of closure to a lesson and that teachers dismiss students, not the bell.

  - For Pre-K–2nd, this is a serious part of the new year. It is extremely important that new teachers KNOW how each child will get home. This often varies for a few months until a routine is established. Making sure that young children get on the right bus or day care van, meet up with a sibling at the school, know where to wait for mom/dad/babysitter/guardian, or get to after-school care is stressful.

  - New students in grades 3–6 may also need assistance.

  - Pick-up procedures and time frames must be clear for new teachers.

- **Emergency Protocols**

  - These protocols include fire drills, shelter in place, evacuation, and live shooter. These alone can cause stress if not read and digested thoroughly as a novice teacher. New teachers need to discuss and practice these events with their students before a school drill or an event occurs. Let them know this and, if need be, help facilitate the first practice.

- **Routines and Procedures**

  - The district and school expectations and routines must always be established and reviewed each year. Special attention should be paid to any new routine or procedure that may have changed from previous years.

  - New teachers must be aware of established discipline procedures and the steps that must be followed. A novice teacher must read and practice the discipline procedures. It is one thing to read them and another to follow through and understand the whys of this system. Sometimes, an observation of another classroom teacher helps solidify how a particular system works.

- Attending a workshop or an after-school professional development hour can help answer a novice teacher's questions.

- **Referrals and Chain of Command**

  - Provide information about the "chain of command" at your school—whom to see for what situation. There is a difference at all grade levels.

  - Typically, a teacher will first talk with a student about the issue and give it time to resolve.

  - If the unwanted behavior continues, a teacher will then contact a parent or guardian and, if necessary, hold a conference with the parent(s) and the student.

  - If the above do not bring about the necessary change in the student, it will be appropriate to involve the next level of staff.

  - Pre-K–6 usually involves the principal or assistant principal and then, if need be, a counselor or psychologist.

  - Grades 7–12 may involve a department chair, dean of students, a counselor, an assistant principal, or the principal.

  - All schools have some type of referral system.

- **Parent Communication**

  - Part of a teacher's responsibilities includes contacting families. Information regarding when they should be contacted, how they should be contacted (phone, email, text), and how to handle the communication will enhance a new teacher's skill set in this area. Being present for and/or offering models to a new teacher for the first few communications are extremely helpful and sometimes necessary.

- **Communications**

  - Each school has expectations about checking physical mailboxes and email. Important information is relayed throughout the school day and novice teachers need to know what is expected in this area. Emails and phone calls are generally expected to be answered within 24–48 hours; the official handbook should clarify this expectation.

- **Professional Responsibilities**

  These questions should be clearly addressed for any new teacher at your school.

  - What does a professional day in your district mean?

  - What time are teachers expected to be on campus?

  - When can teachers leave at the end of the day?

  - Are there other duties during the school day outside of the classroom?

  - What are the expectations for attending IEP, 504, Chronic Illness, and Staff meetings?

  - What is the district policy for sick days and personal days?

  - What other professional responsibilities exist for your school?

- **Open House/Curriculum Night**

  - Knowing what information to present and being prepared to do so in front of parents can be a daunting task. Novice teachers' student teaching experience may not have prepared them for this responsibility.

- Communicate the expectations for these nights. Their appropriate grade level teams (Pre-K–6) or instructional leaders (7–12) may offer assistance. Generally, each teacher or team has a standard presentation so all families hear the same content.

- Time of arrival, dress expectations, sign-in sheets, and time frames all need to be communicated for a successful experience.

- **Field Trips**

  - Due to logistics and safety concerns, this is a complex topic/experience for any teacher to navigate, especially novice teachers. An administrative secretary/assistant usually helps the process. Be clear on how to begin the process for preparing for a field trip. Grade level, individual level, funding, transportation, permission papers, places allowed to go, volunteer vetting, chaperones, and time expectations are all components that must be addressed.

- **Assemblies and Performances**

  - Expectations of attendance by each teacher, whether in class or on prep

  - Seating arrangements for each class

  - Expectations of where teachers should be

  - Behavior expectations and proper etiquette in the gym and/or auditorium

  - Dismissal from the assembly or performance

- **Visiting Teachers, Substitutes**

  - Make sure that novice teachers know the policies and expectations when a visiting teacher/substitute is in the classroom.

  - Communicate expectations for providing seating charts, schedules, emergency evacuation procedures, lesson plans, and behavior systems.

- If there is a paraeducator in the room, teachers should make this information available in their plans so that a visiting teacher knows who the other adult in the room is and what his/her responsibilities are.

- A strong verbal reminder to the students about the courtesies shown for visiting teachers is expected to be made before the teacher's first absence.

- **Pledge, Moment of Silence, Announcements**

  - Be aware of cultural and religious differences.

  - Silence is an expectation and should be established immediately upon the first day of school.

- **Bullying, Peer Mediation**

  - Communicate if your school follows any particular program. Expectations, ramifications, and behavior alignments for the system must be clear.

- **504 Students—Accommodations and Meetings**

  - Educate the novice teacher on the purpose of a 504, documents needed for the meetings, information and observations expected about the student at the meetings, and whether attendance is mandatory.

- **IEP Students—Accommodations and Meetings**

  - Make resources readily available and accessible for students needing assistance.

  - Communicate with new teachers early on who in their classroom has an IEP.

  - Educate your new teachers on the purpose and explanation of an IEP.

  - If a new teacher observes a student who needs help, he/she will need to know how to initiate help for that student, what documents will be needed at the meetings, what kind of documentation will be necessary, and whether attendance is mandatory.

Refer to Chapter 10 for resources that address the wide range of topics presented in this chapter.

ROADBLOCKS and DETOURS

One cannot assume that every school follows the same procedures. With thousands of unique campus settings, expectations, routines, and procedures, it is up to the designated administrator/ leader/coach to establish a communication pathway that will help novice teachers navigate these specific daily routines with success, comfort, and confidence. This will ensure the students' and staff's safety and success—and a strong and smooth start to the school year. How will you determine that fine line of preparing new teachers for their first few weeks in your school without bombarding them? How will you disseminate this information in a timely and efficient manner? As educators, we all know that time is in short supply, but for novice teachers with a never-ending to-do list, time seems even shorter. It is up to principals, assistant principals, instructional leaders, department chairs, and the assigned mentor teacher to establish a positive and caring relationship for these new educators. We cannot afford to lose one due to lack of support!

CHAPTER 3

Educational Overload of Information and Deadlines

Buckle Up!

"The mind is not a vessel to be filled, but a fire to be ignited."

–Plutarch

EXPERIENCE TELLS US

The graph on the following page illustrates a pattern that emerges with new teachers, and we have found this pattern to be evident in our mentoring practice. Not every teacher arrives at each stage at the same time, but the ebb and flow of the first year follows this pattern. While each teacher is unique, knowledge of this universal pattern is helpful when working with new teachers and assisting them in understanding that they are not alone in their challenges.

This graph was originally published by Ellen Moir in the newsletter for the California New Teacher Project, published by the California Department of Education (CDE), 1990. Refer to Chapter 10 for further explanation.

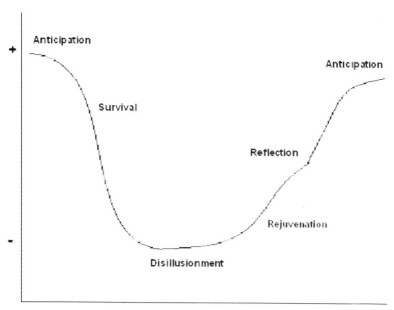

AUG SEPT OCT NOV DEC JAN FEB MAR APR MAY JUN JUL

BEST PRACTICES ... for THE INFINITE FACETS OF A TEACHING DAY

First-year teachers will need support at several levels during weeks six through nine. Either the principal or the principal's designee needs to check in often to provide answers and guidance for the multitude of FIRSTS that a novice teacher faces. For new teachers, disillusionment at this point in the year results from the reality that they must constantly juggle any number of new skills. Planning, obtaining materials, grading, posting, responding to other obligations, and finding personal time can collide and become overwhelming. Other obligations can include graduate classes, coaching, clubs, committees, attendance at events, and second jobs.

Either the principal or the principal's designee needs to check in often to provide answers and guidance for the multitude of FIRSTS that a novice teacher faces.

19

New teachers need continuous feedback that is not part of the official observation and assessment cycle. A lot can be observed by dropping in during the first and last five minutes of class, or any five minutes in between. Communicating via email, a written note, or a brief one-on-one exchange can address both what is going well and what needs attention at that point in time. Being afforded the opportunity to observe the class of a veteran teacher who has mastered the skills you believe a new teacher may need to consider can be invaluable for a novice.

Some ways in which this can occur are:

- The principal, assistant principal, dean, instructional coach, or special area teachers can cover part of new teachers' classes.
- New teachers can use their prep time to observe another teacher's class.
- Professional development funds can be used to pay a teacher or substitute to cover new teachers' classes.
- New teachers can use part or all of a personal day to observe a variety of teachers.
- Veteran teachers can volunteer to cover new teachers' classes during their prep.

The following are areas for guiding and supporting your new teachers during weeks six through nine:

- **Communication**
  - Parent-Teacher Conferences—Scheduling
    - Who is in charge of the master conference schedule?
    - How is the scheduling information disseminated? When and where do conferences take place?
    - Are conferences scheduled, or do parents float from one teacher to another? (secondary)

- How do you assist parents in managing conference schedules when there are multiple children at the same school?
- How do teachers access the language line/translator?
- Are phone conferences acceptable for parents who cannot attend?

■ Holding the Conference

- What are the exact expectations of comportment and attire?
- How will new teachers prepare and accumulate the entire picture of each child's ability over the last nine weeks and capture the essence of accomplishment or lack thereof in a unique package?
- How will you communicate the idea of a "sandwich conference," which entails starting with the student's strengths, discussing areas of concern, and ending with praise and a plan for improvement?
- How does a teacher end a conference that exceeds the designated time when others are waiting?
- How does a teacher request additional time in the future if the conference indicates it is necessary?
- How does a teacher handle a parent who is defensive or threatening?
- Does the teacher know whom to contact should a conference derail?
- How does a teacher include support personnel (reading specialist, speech, OT, PT, nurse) to attend the conferences?
- Reiterate the need for communication with parents, especially when there are issues with the student; this can occur at any time, from the first week through the end of the year.

- **Grading**
  - Grades
    - How many assessments are expected to record a legitimate grade by both mid-quarter and end of the quarter?
    - When is the due date for mid-quarter grades?
    - What are the expectations of communication with parents—a grade lower than a C?
    - When are quarter grades due?
    - How are grades posted?
    - Are any students falling far below expectations? What interventions are being used?
  - Assessments
    - What kinds of assessments are novice teachers using? Formative? Summative? Benchmark? Projects?
    - Grading results—How many As? How many Fs? Do novice teachers' grades reflect a fair assessment of the work?
    - Have grade levels come to a consensus on the summative/end-of-semester assessments in conjunction with the standards?
    - What do novice teachers need to know about semester exam preparation? Are there common department assessments? Do new teachers know how to prepare a multiple-choice/project-based semester assessment that reflects 18 weeks of learning?
    - Will their assessment be aligned with the grade level/subject matter/state standards?
    - Are grading practices aligned with those of other colleagues? Have grading expectations been communicated with the new teachers?
    - How many grades comprise a quarter grade?

- ◆ How often do grades need to be posted and updated?
- ◆ What percentages are assigned to varying assessments and assignments?
- ◆ Are appropriate rubrics being implemented?

- **Classroom Management**
  - ▦ Are there any major challenges regarding student behavior/attitude/motivation?
  - ▦ How is the teacher engaging the students throughout instruction?
  - ▦ Is technology being incorporated into daily lesson design?

Refer to Chapter 10 for additional resources on parent conferences, rubrics, assessment, and feedback.

ROADBLOCKS AND DETOURS

As the first quarter approaches completion, first-year teachers are often overwhelmed with the associated demands and deadlines that it brings. Students are getting comfortable and may be behaving differently as a result. New teachers are observing varying levels of skill, motivation, and productivity in their students. Novice teachers are realizing that their planning and organization are daily responsibilities. If their grading and posting have piled up, there can be some panic in finalizing quarter grades.

Parent conferences are often part of this time of year as well. One major challenge of parent conferences for elementary-age students is not understanding how to schedule the conferences far enough out to accommodate all families.

We cannot state strongly enough how vital it is for new teachers to have your support at this critical time of year. This is a juncture at which new teachers can thrive with confidence at having completed the first quarter or be discouraged with their career choice.

CHAPTER 4

Implementing Lessons and Assessments

Attaining Results in the First Semester

"Education is a lifelong journey whose destination expands as you travel."

–Jim Stovall

EXPERIENCE TELLS US

The idea of backward design comes from Wiggins and McTighe and suggests that learning experiences should be planned with the final assessment in mind. One starts with the end—the desired results—and then derives the curriculum from the evidence of learning (performances) dictated by the standard and the teaching needed to equip students to perform (Wiggins & McTighe, 2000). By beginning with the end in mind, teachers are able to avoid the common problem of planning forward from one unit to another, only to find at the end of the semester that critical lessons have not been solidified. This can result in some students being prepared for the final assessment while others are not.

BEST PRACTICES ... FOR DISTRICT CURRICULUM AND STATE STANDARDS

Novice teachers need guidance and direction to see beyond what is in front of them today. With the beginning of the second quarter and the end of the semester in sight, it is a good time for them to think about "beginning with the end in mind." This means they must understand the scope of the district's curriculum maps and how they align with state standards to ensure they are capturing all lessons, information, and instruction that needs to take place within the designated semester, year, class, or subject area. Thinking with the end in sight helps any teacher understand how to fully and effectively scaffold, what prior knowledge is needed, and where to attach previous learning to pinpoint accurate lesson designs.

Elementary Assessments

- Help teachers prepare for early childhood assessments (DIBELS, DRA) or a formative assessment that has been approved by your district.

- Make teachers aware of the testing windows for your district.

- Understand how to properly prepare and fully instruct on the delivery of the assessments.

- Communicate that any assessment not delivered with integrity and fidelity is invalid.

- Teach novice teachers how to weave components of test preparation through daily lessons rather than standalone teaching for testing. This is where backward design fits in and is important to understand. New teachers should consult the Standards-Based Curriculum Guide to ensure all expectations of grade level learning are being met.

Secondary First-Semester Exams

- Delegate someone to oversee that the new teachers' exams properly assess student learning for the semester and coincide with the department's common semester assessments.

- Check in to see that new teachers have a plan for reviewing and preparing their students for the semester exam.
- Ensure that new teachers are aware of the pacing to complete the semester curriculum.
- Ensure that new teachers' exams and semester grades are weighted in accordance with departmental policy.

Ending the Semester

- Communicate what is required to complete the semester, such as posting grades, reports, classroom condition, etc.
- Clarify what is required to shut down the classroom for the winter break. Are there theft issues? Should personal items go home? Does equipment require an extra layer of lock-up? Do thermostats need adjustment during the break?
- Parental contact—failures/credits
  - Does the student (secondary) continue in the class if their first-semester grade is an F?
  - Will any schedules change?
  - What happens if a student wants to drop the class at the end of the semester? What are the policies?
- Communicate any other deadlines your school or district has at this time of year.

Thinking Ahead

- Suggest that the teacher find time to plan for the first week back, including having materials and copies organized. In this way, when the teacher leaves for break, he/she can truly enjoy the time away from work and still be prepared for the students upon their return.

- Communicate if there is a day that the building will be open during break(s).

- Suggest that the new teacher carve out a set time to work over the break, IF he/she wants to, and then stick with that plan—one day? Two half-days? Encourage them to really take time away to do what re-energizes them.

- Celebrate the completion of one full semester of teaching!

- Provide a means for new teachers to reflect on their successes in the first semester and modifications needed to begin the second semester competently. Refer to Chapter 10 for more ideas on the reflection process.

Refer to Chapter 10 for a variety of resources on lesson design.

ROADBLOCKS AND DETOURS

This time of year, both students and teachers are engaged in holiday activities. Completing the quarter and the semester requires planning and organization, as some novice teachers are still working day to day. The deadlines of grading, finalizing grades, communicating with parents whose students are failing, and preparing for winter break can be daunting.

For elementary school, instructional time sometimes gets away because of holiday celebrations. Every day counts, and actual teaching time must not be sacrificed at this time of year. New teachers may not realize the behavior problems that can ensue from a less-organized classroom, so they truly need guidance in this area at holiday time.

Communicate the expectations of holiday gift giving with teachers. In some elementary schools, teachers give small items to each of their students—Scholastic books, pencils, stickers, candy, plastic cups filled with goodies, etc. Take this opportunity to make novice teachers aware of the

The deadlines of grading, finalizing grades, communicating with parents whose students are failing, and preparing for winter break can be daunting.

27

district guidelines for receiving gifts from families and to heighten their awareness of those students who do not celebrate the holidays.

CHAPTER 5

Curriculum Goals and Instruction

Exploring the Landscape!

"The good is, like nature, an immense landscape in which man advances through centuries of exploration."

–José Ortega y Gassett

EXPERIENCE TELLS US

When class resumes in January, teachers need to revisit the expectations for both the class and student behavior. The time spent on this should be appropriate for the grade level of the students. Second-semester goals and objectives should be communicated with a plan for continued development and rigorous implementation. With this in mind, students must be aware that attendance, participation, engagement, and growth are paramount for a successful academic second semester.

BEST PRACTICES ... FOR BEGINNING THE SECOND SEMESTER

Each part of the year has a different ebb and flow. One advantage of our profession is the opportunity to begin anew and progress. A new school year starts a brand-new journey. Depending on a novice teacher's skill set, the beginning of the second semester can have a fresh look or can be a continuation of a solid journey. By this point, it can be assumed that an administrator has been observing and that someone has been intervening and mentoring so that the second semester can have a smoother start than the first day of school. Hopefully, this semester will find your novice teachers more settled into their practice and will allow deeper thought about their lessons and assessments. As stated in the Preface, guiding novice teachers through what is required during different times of the year is essential.

> *By this point, it can be assumed that an administrator has been observing and that someone has been intervening and mentoring so that the second semester can have a smoother start than the first day of school.*

Refer to Chapter 10 for resources on assessment.

The following guidelines are important items to consider and execute as the second semester begins:

- Continued observation and consistent feedback need to occur during the second semester.

- Curriculum goals need to be reviewed and laid out for the second semester with the crucial support the new teachers may need.

- Developing an engaging topic or activity for the new semester will help motivate students upon their return from break. Has anyone conferred with new teachers about this?

- The administration/coach/mentor needs to check to determine how the teachers' goals are progressing in terms of the district evaluation system.

- Continued support in solidifying and implementing their goals and recording the results is paramount for novice teachers to document academic growth in their classroom.

- Classroom routines and/or procedures may need to be reestablished or restructured for consistent management success. This could include changing seat assignments, room arrangement or any other modification.

- Secondary teachers will need to know your school's registration process and timeline for the following year.

- Secondary teachers will need to know about requirements and recommendations from one grade/course level to the next. This pertains to 7th and 8th grades, as well as to high school students.

- New teachers will need feedback and guidance to evaluate their class and pinpoint the needs, both from the students' perspective and from the administrator's viewpoint, regarding their delivery of instruction.

- The expectations for new teachers must remain high. Their lessons need to be engaging and based on 21st-century skills.

- New teachers need to be shown a variety of formative assessments so they can assess their students throughout each lesson. Providing resources for them to distinguish between formative and summative assessments will benefit both them and their students. Chapter 10 defines the two types of assessments and includes a variety of specific examples of each. Many new teachers are unaware of the functions of these two types of assessments.

ROADBLOCKS AND DETOURS

Some areas of the country may experience the "winter blues." Novice teachers will require added encouragement to maintain their energy and provide meaningful and engaging lessons for their students.

For some states, this is also the time of year when state testing is near. Both teachers and students are held accountable for testing results. New teachers will need information about administering the tests. They also will require guidance regarding what they need to teach before the test is administered as well as specifics on administering the actual test. We recommend that there be two proctors in each testing room. New teachers will also need sufficient materials throughout the year to practice for state-mandated tests, both paper and digital.

Watch for frustration on the part of the teachers regarding the interruptions and outside expectations beyond their classroom work as they continue to prepare for the necessary learning to take place.

CHAPTER 6

Observing the Learning Patterns of the Students

Watching the Signs and Checking the Map

"Every life is a canvas and every interaction is a brush, therefore we'd be wise to consider how we handle the paint."

–Craig D. Lounsbrough

EXPERIENCE TELLS US

By the third quarter, new teachers should be aware that their students' strengths, weaknesses, and learning styles vary greatly. Learner variability should be addressed as the novice teacher begins to understand differentiation and each student's individual learning style. Teachers can use a wide variety of tools to provide a differentiated environment that meets the individual needs of students and is culturally responsive. "By gaining insights into how the brain works—and how students actually learn—teachers will be able to create their own solutions to the classroom challenges they face and improve their practice" (Neuroscience & the Classroom: Making Connections—Annenberg Learner, www.learner.org/courses/neuroscience/).

Until now, new teachers have most likely focused on lesson planning, pacing, and grading. This is an optimal time of year for new teachers to look at a few students in depth and determine how to reach them. Adjusting lessons to meet the learning styles of a few students will result in differentiated lessons that will reach most students in the class.

Refer to Chapter 10 for resources on learner profiles and learner differences.

BEST PRACTICES ... FOR COMMUNICATING EXPECTATIONS AS THE YEAR PROGRESSES

By the middle of the third quarter, middle and high school students have made their choices of classes and registered for the following year. Spring break is in the mix, and summer break is becoming part of the students' discussion. For all grade levels, this is the time of year when new teachers should be concerned about completing the curriculum and whether their students will be prepared for the next level.

The following points are important to consider at this point in the year:

- Make sure the state standards have been addressed, both up to this point and going forward. Check on pacing—what needs to be completed by the end of the year?

- Prepare new teachers to understand that all curriculum must be acknowledged, taught, and reviewed for all students to be well prepared for the upcoming assessments and the next academic level.

- Communicate once again the importance of and procedures for parent-teacher conferences. This is an opportune time to make sure new teachers have touched base with all families and those in particular whose child(ren) is/are struggling or having difficulties in each class or subject—depending on grade level. Are there students who continue to struggle? Are there students who are not being challenged? Are there students who are not going to pass the class? What interventions are being implemented? Has the new teacher sought guidance from the social worker, counselor, special education coordinator, psychologist, or nurse on campus to obtain a comprehensive view of the struggling students' strengths and challenges?

- Have new teachers examine possibilities for what students might do as a capstone activity. Caution new secondary teachers to have major projects due before May, so as not to overload the students and conflict with AP tests and second-semester exams.

- Communicate the expectations for second-semester exams for secondary and district tests for elementary. Are there departmental assessments? Are there common assessments? Does the new teacher need to create his/her own? Now is the time to guide new teachers in thinking ahead. Your support and communication are particularly needed here, as it can be difficult for new teachers to think forward; they are usually taking care of what is right in front of them during their first year.

- Urge new teachers to continue encouraging and motivating their students to achieve. For some students, passing with a D is a major achievement and not a failure.

ROADBLOCKS AND DETOURS

The third quarter is when myriad issues arise. New teachers need to have specific support in designing and implementing engaging and meaningful lessons.It is crucial to encourage new teachers to maintain their energy by achieving a balance between their work and personal lives. Their assessments should be on target and data driven. Data analysis, interpretation, and implementation are crucial components for new teachers to develop and understand. Data will not be addressed here; it is a topic for another book. New teachers will need information and appropriate support to manage the formats for whatever testing situations are part of your school this semester. We cannot stress how important it is to familiarize new teachers with your protocols throughout the year. What is muscle memory for veterans may be unknown to novices.

New teachers need to have specific support in designing and imple- menting engaging and meaningful lessons.

As stated in Chapter 3, feedback for new teachers is critical to their growth. Acknowledging what new teachers are accomplishing at this time of year can provide the connection and encouragement that motivate them to remain in the teaching profession.

CHAPTER 7

Have the Learning Indicators Been Achieved?

How to End the Year and Reach the Destination

"Don't cry because it's over, smile because it happened."

–Dr. Seuss

EXPERIENCE TELLS US

Spring in any classroom or school must be experienced to comprehend the scope of activities and deadlines that exist for each teacher. New teachers cannot anticipate what spring is like, so communication and support from the administration are vital at this time of year.

The distractions that may chip away at students' academic focus are numerous:

- Elementary
  - Spring break
  - Warm weather
  - State testing

- ■ Spring performances
- ■ Summer vacations
- ● Secondary
  - ■ Spring break
  - ■ Warm weather
  - ■ State testing
  - ■ Spring performances
  - ■ AP exams
  - ■ Second-semester exams
  - ■ Prom
  - ■ Deadlines
  - ■ Graduation
  - ■ Summer jobs
  - ■ Summer vacations

Even though most of the curriculum has been taught by the middle of the fourth quarter, there is still a lot of time to continue the learning process. The review of subject matter and completion of all curriculum assigned for this year's instruction should continue. Adhering to the core curriculum at all costs sets up the direction for a successful end of year. Bell to bell teaching is paramount to ensure that the integrity of classroom management, motivation and instruction are maintained until the last minute of the year.

> *Bell-to-bell teaching is paramount to ensure that the integrity of classroom management, motivation and instruction are maintained until the last minute of the year.*

BEST PRACTICES ... FOR COMPLETING THE ACADEMIC YEAR

With all that spring brings, it can and should be a time of celebration! Encourage new teachers to consider the memorable lessons and the skills that have been acquired this year. How might they celebrate all the learning that has taken place because of their instruction? Rally them to return to units with a depth that time constraints prohibited during the year. Suggest that they assign a culminating activity that facilitates collaboration with the students and offers insight into their grasp of the curriculum. Younger grades might write a letter to the next group of students coming into that grade. Upper grades could create a timeline of the year's best learning experiences. Teachers can detail the hardest lessons and have the students help design ideas that would help the next class.

Other possibilities include:

- Review and applaud the year's academic growth—appropriate for all levels
- Capstone projects—secondary
- Second-semester exam review and preparation—secondary

Proposing summer **professional development** for new teachers is something you can do to help them in areas where they need additional training or to enhance skills that you observe to be their strengths. Professional development may take place within the district, as a university class, or in the form of a conference or workshop provided by professional organizations. Making consistent professional development a part of their responsibilities will rejuvenate teachers' passion for teaching and their own desire to learn.

Refer to Chapter 10 for resources on ways to end the school year successfully.

ROADBLOCKS AND DETOURS

New teachers will require a tremendous amount of support to stay on track and manage their obligations so they do not end their year in a stressful frenzy. End-of-year responsibilities include:

- State testing (in some states)
- AP testing and the resulting absences that occur in other classes
- Second-semester exams
- ESL proficiency testing
- Posting final grades
- Building checkout lists
- Separating the class
- Early exams prepared for special education and 504 students
- Preparing the classroom for summer—taking down posters and bulletin boards, securing media and personal items, submitting repair lists
- Ordering materials for the following year

Assemblies and end-of-year activities can detract from the curriculum when learning must be sustained. The academic year can be brought to thoughtful closure with conscientious planning and insight about review and reflection. Suggesting a folder for "end-of-year responsibilities"—either digital or paper—will help new teachers stay organized and meet their deadlines.

CHAPTER 8

Thinking Ahead—Reflection
Adjusting the Mirrors

"Mind is a flexible mirror, adjust it,
to see a better world."

–Amit Ray

RESEARCH TELLS US

When new teachers reflect on the strengths and modifications of the school year, they have the opportunity to see where they can improve for the following year. They can affirm what has gone well and build on that success. Reflection is an intentional competence that enables new teachers to identify their best practices, refine areas that need attention, and avoid those difficult situations they may have encountered in their inaugural year. Continuous reflective practice is paramount in education. Each year, we have the opportunity to start anew. Refer to Chapter 10 for references on reflection for both teachers and students.

For many teachers, summer is an opportune time to take advantage of professional development opportunities offered by the district, universities, or in the form of a conference or workshop. This can allow dedicated time to really capitalize on their learning. This time can also be used to rework an area of instructional delivery, management, or organization. Improving these areas can ultimately strengthen and shore up new teachers' proficiency.

BEST PRACTICES ... FOR ENHANCING THEIR CRAFT

Encourage new teachers to use your observations, walk-throughs, evaluation(s), and their own reflections to determine the areas they would like

Reflection is an intentional competence that enables new teachers to identify their best practices, refine areas that need attention, and avoid those difficult situations they may have encountered in their inaugural year.

to work on to create a solid start in year two of their teaching career. Help them prioritize no more than three areas, and urge them to take a class, attend a seminar, collaborate with a proficient colleague, and/or research online to gain information that will guide their growth. Oftentimes, refining a few key components of their teaching will result in the resolution of many other issues at the same time.

"Sharpen the saw means preserving and enhancing the greatest asset you have—you." Sharpen the Saw is Habit 7 in "The 7 Habits of Highly Effective People" by Stephen R. Covey. New teachers who recognize the value of continually sharpening their personal and professional saws will be able to achieve balance in their lives and productivity in their classrooms. It will, in fact, be vital to them remaining in education.

As new teachers reflect on their year, encourage them to look toward the first two weeks of the new school year. Preparing opening-of-school materials prior to the official start of school will already have them thinking ahead to the rest of the new school year.

ROADBLOCKS AND DETOURS

Not reflecting or acting on what is needed to move forward will be detrimental to new teachers as well as their students, both in the following year and in years to come. Continually developing, revising, and refining professional practices is vital to keeping our classrooms vibrant, current, and engaging for our students. Reflection and professional development are expectations that must be communicated and become part of teachers' continual growth.

The following quote from Hiam Ginott's "Teacher and Child" fittingly expresses what each novice teacher must decide for his/her students each and every day:

"I've come to a frightening conclusion that I am the decisive element in the classroom. It's my personal approach that creates the climate. It's my daily mood that makes the weather. As a teacher, I possess a tremendous power to make a child's life miserable or joyous. I can be a tool of torture or an instrument of inspiration. I can humiliate or humor, hurt or heal. In all situations, it is my response that decides whether a crisis will be escalated or de-escalated and a child humanized or dehumanized."

We are hopeful that the content of this book will allow you to guide and support your new teachers so they may find their own voice to inspire our nation's children.

CHAPTER 9

Mentoring Other Staff Members

Shifting All the Gears

"In this district you either teach or you support those who do."

–Dr. Jim Jurs
Retired Superintendent
Paradise Valley Unified School District #69

EXPERIENCE TELLS US

We need to invest time, training, and resources in our support staff, as they are an integral part of the entire learning environment for faculty and students. They are the backbone behind the inner working of a school—the "unsung heroes."

School support staff includes a variety of staff members who provide specialized instructional support as well as support to students while they use school facilities. They play an important role in ensuring students are learning in a safe and supportive learning environment. They can foster positive, trusting relationships with students and improve school climate by encouraging parents/guardians and family involvement in education. Because students connect with them on many occasions throughout the school day, support staff can model positive behavior and send positive messages to students.

We need to invest time, training, and resources in our support staff, as they are an integral part of the entire learning environment for faculty and students. They are the backbone behind the inner working of a school—the "unsung heroes."

Support staff may include, but are not limited to:

- Administrative Assistant
- Attendance Clerk
- Coaches
- Custodian
- Duty Aide
- Hearing Specialist
- Nurse
- Occupational Therapist
- Paraprofessional
- Parent Liaison
- Physical Therapist
- Records Secretary
- Security
- Social Worker
- Vision Specialist

BEST PRACTICES ... FOR INVESTING IN SUPPORT STAFF

All new support staff will need the following information communicated to them clearly:

- School vision and mission statement
- Campus climate
- Special needs/1–1 and duty aides
- Their role in supporting what teachers do
- Their role in interacting with students
- Their role in managing student behavior
- Their role in commanding respectful behavior
- Name of their supervisor
- Daily work schedule
- Traits and experiences they bring to the job
- Job description/expectations (different for each position)
- Introduction of new support staff at staff meetings

Ownership of the entire academic environment empowers all staff members to be an integral part of its fluid interactions.

Refer to Chapter 10 for resources regarding support staff.

ROADBLOCKS AND DETOURS

Lack of communication and training of new support staff will impede the continuity of the instructional day. Novice teachers and support staff should have an understanding of each other's roles and how each impacts the other. Work on ways to increase collaboration for positive efforts toward an enriching school environment.

CHAPTER 10

Charging the Battery

Using the Resources

"If you don't know where you are going,
you'll end up somewhere else."

–Goethe

This chapter offers specific resources to reinforce the information presented in chapters 1–9. It is not meant to be a complete rendering of resources, but rather a place for administrators to begin to offer additional support to new teachers. Reading an article or watching a video will not resolve the challenges that new teachers face. However, combining these resources with guidance for effective execution will result in teachers developing the necessary skills and confidence that will lead to their students' academic achievement.

Disclaimer: As authors, we have done everything in our power to ensure all sites are live and working. We cannot guarantee they will be maintained in the future.

Each chapter contains specific resources for the topics addressed in that chapter.

The following sites have a wealth of information on every topic in education.

Edutopia –https://www.edutopia.org

NEA–http://www.nea.org

National PTA –http://www.pta.org

CHAPTER 1

Classroom Management Resources

Creating a positive environment for learning; developing relationships with students; establishing, communicating, and following through with routines and procedures; and presenting engaging relevant lessons are all ways in which teachers establish a well-managed classroom. An abundance of articles, videos, and blogs are available online to assist new teachers with these fundamental components of teaching. New teachers will also strengthen their skills through their individual personalities, collaborating with colleagues, and getting effective feedback from administrators.

- ★ **33 Ways to Start the Year**
  http://www.nea.org/tools/33-ways-to-start-the-first-year-off-right.html

- ★ **Building Positive Classrooms**
  http://www.ascd.org/publications/educational-leadership/sept08/vol66/num01/Seven-Strategies-for-Building-Positive-Classrooms.aspx

- ★ **Classroom Culture vs. Classroom Management**
  https://www.teachingchannel.org/blog/2015/08/25/class-culture-vs-class-mgmnt/?utm_source=newsletter20150829/

★ **Classroom Tips for Novice Teachers**
https://www.edutopia.org/blog/classroom-management-tips-novice-teachers-rebecca-alber

★ **Developing Clear Classroom Rules and Expectations**
http://k12teacherstaffdevelopment.com/tlb/benefits-of-developing-cl

★ **Fred Jones**
http://www.fredjones.com

★ **Harry Wong –courses; pay**
http://www.harrywong.com

★ **Managing Instructional Time**
http://www.ascd.org/publications/.../Managing-Instructional-Time.aspx

★ **PBIS –Classroom Management**
http://www.pbisworld.com

★ **Starting the School Year Right**
http://www.educationworld.com/a_curr/columnists/jones/jones019.

★ **The First Two Weeks of School**
http://www.teach-nology.com/ideas/start_year/

CHAPTER 2

Many of the ideas presented in this chapter are specific to districts, corporations, and schools and this will need to be addressed within the context of your information system.

We have chosen the following resources to provide insight into the administrator's role in a new teacher's success and to provide specific information that will support new teachers with the topics in this chapter.

★ **504 Education Plan**
   http://kidshealth.org/en/parents/504-teachers.html

★ **Effective Teams: The Key to Transforming Schools**
   https://www.edutopia.org/blog/teacher-teams-transform-schools-elena-aguilar

★ **Maintaining Discipline**
   http://www.nea.org/tools/31410.htm

★ **Parent Communication Tips**
   https://www.thoughtco.com/tips-for-highly-successful-parent-teacher-communication-3194676

★ **Rethinking Difficult Parents**
   https://www.edutopia.org/blog/rethinking-difficult-parents-allen-mendler

★ **School Leaders: 6 Strategies for Retaining New Teachers**
   https://www.edutopia.org/blog/school-leaders-six-strategies-retaining-new-teachers-elena-aguilar

★ **The IEP Meeting**
   https://www.verywell.com/understanding-iep-team-meetings-2162678

★ **Three Ways Administrators Can Foster Teachers Growth**
   http://greatergood.berkeley.edu/article/item/3_ways_administrators_can_foster_teachers_growth

★ **What I Wish I Knew As A First Year Teacher**
   https://www.edutopia.org/blog/what-i-wish-id-known-new-teacher-elena-aguilar

CHAPTER 3 _____

★ **Phases of a First-Year Teacher By Ellen Moir**

This article was originally written for publication in the newsletter for the California New Teacher Project, published by the California Department of Education (CDE), 1990

1. PHASES OF TEACHING—CONDENSED

The first year of teaching is challenging and overwhelming for novice teachers. It is also very challenging and overwhelming for district, schools and administrators to find the time to support and retain new teachers. Ellen Moir (Founder and Director of the New Teacher Center, Santa Cruz) has developed a diagram explaining the phases that most, not all, new teachers experience their first and possibly second and third years of teaching.

Anticipation phase is where the new teachers get keys to their OWN classroom and are so excited, yet anxious about this being their first experience alone as a teacher. This excitement continues as they begin the year.

The Survival phase comes next and is a wake-up call to the overwhelming amount of expectations and paperwork that are placed on top of teaching the students. Curriculum needs to be aligned with state standards, lesson plans to address differentiation, grading and, if time is left, try and have a life of their own.

Disillusionment phase! begins 6-8 weeks in with stress, non-stop teaching, first quarter grades, open house/curriculum night and parent conferences. Some are questioning if this was what they thought teaching would be like. They question their management styles, their delivery of lessons, and the amount of work (sometimes 60+ hours a week) to maintain the daily routines.

Rejuvenation phase starts the beginning of January when they have had some time to resume a normal life routine, re-establish friendships, no time constraints and a time to come up for air at a slower pace. They have a better handle on expectations, routines, behavior management, and curriculum pacing.

Reflection phase usually begins in May, as the new teachers have a chance to reflect on what went right and what needs to be massaged for the following year. They can look forward to what their second year will look like and hopefully a sense of having the first year under their belt. Administrators need to be aware of this cycle, when recognized and validated; new teachers know this is a normal process-all new teachers experience.

2. GRADING TIPS, RUBRICS

★ **Designing rubrics**
http://www.cmu.edu/teaching/designteach/teach/rubrics.html

★ **How Rubrics Help**
https://www.edutopia.org/assessment-guide-rubrics

★ **Using Rubrics to Promote Thinking and Learning**
http://www.ascd.org/publications/educational-leadership/feb00/vol57/num05/Using-Rubrics-to-Promote-Thinking-and-Learning.aspx

3. PARENT CONFERENCES

Although parents are a critical component of a child's education, 100 percent attendance at conferences does not usually occur. Teachers need to understand what it takes to prepare materials and information about each student for the conferences. They need to be able to reach out multiple times to parents/guardians to try to arrange a conference, whether in person, by phone, or by email. Drastic measures could also entail a home visit with a counselor, dean, or another teacher going along with the teacher of record.

★ **Parent Teacher Conferences**
http://www.nea.org/tools/parent-teacherconferences.html

★ **Tips for Parents**
http://www.thelearningcommunity.us/resources-by-
format/tips-for-parents/parent-teacher-conferences.aspx

4. ASSESSMENT

★ **Assessment in the Classroom**
http://assessment.tki.org.nz/Assessment-in-the-
classroom
★ **Classroom Assessment Techniques**
https://cft.vanderbilt.edu/guides-sub-pages/cats/
★ **Formative and Summative Assessment**
http://fcit.usf.edu/assessment/basic/basica.html
★ **How Classroom Assessment Improves Learning**
http://www.ascd.org/publications/educational-
leadership/feb03/vol60/num05/How-Classroom-Assessm
ents-Improve-Learning.aspx

5. FEEDBACK

★ **7 Steps to Effective Feedback**
http://connectedprincipals.com/archives/6335
★ **The Art of Giving Feedback**
http://blogs.edweek.org/teachers/coaching_teachers
/2013/03/giving_feedback.html

CHAPTER 4 _____

Ideas for K–12 lesson design are limitless, as lesson design factors
include grade level, curriculum, individual scope and sequence, class
size, skill level, personality of the teacher and the students, and
resources available within the school.

★ **20 Movement Activities for the Elementary Classroom**
http://gazette.teachers.net/gazette/wordpress/leah-
davies/movement-games/

★ **ASCD's Information on Teacher Reflection**
http://www.ascd.org/publications/educational-leader
ship/feb09/vol66/num05/Fostering-Reflection.aspx

★ **Backward Design**
http://www.fitnyc.edu/files/pdfs/Backward_design.pdf

★ **Move Your Body, Grow Your Brain**
https://www.edutopia.org/blog/move-body-grow-brain-
donna-wilson

★ **Movement Activities for the Secondary Classroom**
http://inservice.ascd.org/four-movement-activities-for-s
econdary-classrooms/

★ **Movement Strategies For All Ages**
http://ncsdmentors.weebly.com/uploads/9/6/2/9/9629075/
descriptionsofstrategies.pdf

★ **Project Based Learning**
https://www.edutopia.org/project-based-learning

★ **Socratic Method of Teaching**
http://www.criticalthinking.org/pages/socratic-
teaching/606

★ **Teaching Critical Thinking With Questioning
Strategies**
http://www.ascd.org/publications/educational-
leadership/mar10/vol67/num06/Teaching-Critical-Readin
g-with-Questioning-Strategies.aspx

★ **TED Talk –There is No Average**
https://www.youtube.com/watch?v=4eBmyttcfU4

★ **The First Five Minutes of a Lesson**
https://www.edutopia.org/blog/first-five-minutes-richard-
curwin

- ★ **Time on Task**
  https://feaweb.org/time-on-task-a-teaching-strategy-that-accelerates-learning
- ★ **Universal Design for Learning**
  http://www.udlcenter.org/aboutudl/whatisudl

CHAPTER 5

Many new teachers do not enter the profession with an adequate amount of skill and practice in preparing assessments and understanding how to measure student growth. This is an area in which teachers need guidance, knowledge, and development.

- ★ **Comprehensive Assessment**
  https://www.edutopia.org/comprehensive-assessment-introduction
- ★ **Five Fantastic Formative Assessment Tools**
  https://www.edutopia.org/blog/5-fast-formative-assessment-tools-vicki-davis
- ★ **Formative Assessment Resources**
  https://www.teachingchannel.org/blog/2015/03/04/formative-assessment-resources/?utm_ source=newsletter20161008/
- ★ **Formative and Summative Assessments**
  https://www.amle.org/BrowsebyTopic/WhatsNew/WNDet/TabId/270/ArtMID/888/ArticleID/286/Formative-and-Summative-Assessments-in-the Classroom. aspx
- ★ **The Exit Slip**
  https://www.edutopia.org/blog/formative-assessment-xit-slip-rebecca-alber

CHAPTER 6

Recognizing the individual needs of all learners and how they acquire knowledge and adapt to the delivery and retention of instruction is a paramount tool that new teachers must develop over time.

- ★ **All Kinds of Minds**
  http://www.allkindsofminds.org/cs-aaron
- ★ **Designing Lessons for Unique Learners**
  https://www.teachingchannel.org/blog/2014/02/24/udl-for-unique-learners/
- ★ **Differentiated Instruction**
  https://www.edutopia.org/blogs/tag/differentiated-instruction
- ★ **Discover Your Preferred Learning Style**
  http://www.brainboxx.co.uk/a3_aspects/pages/vak_quest.htm
- ★ **How Learning Profiles Can Strengthen Your Teaching**
  https://www.edutopia.org/blog/learning-profiles-john-mccarthy
- ★ **New Teacher Survival Guide: Differentiating Instruction**
  https://www.teachingchannel.org/videos/differentiating-instruction
- ★ **Resources for Differentiated Instruction**
  https://www.edutopia.org/search-results?search=differentiation
- ★ **Self Assessment for Learning Style**
  http://www.educationplanner.org/students/self-assessments/index.shtml

CHAPTER 7 _____

Just as beginning an academic year requires planning and preparation, so does completing the academic year calls for deliberate thought to bring closure to the year.

- ★ **A Teacher's Guide for Ending the School Year**
  http://www.teach-nology.com/themes/holidays/endofyear/

★ **Administrators Preparing for the End of the Year**
https://www.powerschool.com/administrators-can-prepare-end-school-year/

★ **End of Year Activities K-8**
https://www.scholastic.com/teachers/collections/teaching-content/end-year-activities-0/

★ **Engaging End of the Year Project Ideas**
https://www.edutopia.org/blog/end-of-year-engaging-projects-rebecca-alber?utm_source=Silverpop
Mailing&utm_medium=email&utm_campaign=051017%
20enews%20thoughtprovoking&utm_content=&utm_ter
m=fea4hed&spMailingID=17194455&spUserID=MzYx
MjM0OTA5ODgzS0&spJobID=1020786881&spReportI
d=MTAyMDc4Njg4MQS2

★ **Tips for Preparing for the End of the Year**
https://www.teachercreated.com/blog/2009/06/tips-preparing-for-the-end-of-the-school-year/

CHAPTER 8 _____

Although these resources on reflection are presented at the end of the book, constant reflection is a habit that all new teachers should establish and practice during the entire school year and beyond.

★ **5 Reflective End-of-Year Activities**
https://www.teachingchannel.org/blog/2014/05/23/reflecti
ve-end-of-year-activities/?utm_source
=newsletter20160527/

★ **Fostering Reflection**
http://www.ascd.org/publications/educational-leadership/feb09/vol66/num05/Fostering-Reflection.aspx

★ **Student and Teacher Reflections**
http://www.megandredge.com/11-end-of-year-reflection-questions-for-your-students/

★ **Teacher Reflection Template and Stems**
https://myportfolio.school.nz/group/reflection-and-registration/teacher-reflection-template

CHAPTER 9

★ **School Support Staff**
https://safesupportivelearning.ed.gov/training-technical-assistance/roles/school-support-staff

★ **Staff Management**
https://www.forbes.com/forbes/welcome/?toURL=https://www.forbes.com/2010/06/30/mentor-coach-executive-training-leadership-managing-ccl.html&refURL=https://search.yahoo.com/&referrer=https://search.yahoo.com/

★ **The Importance of Education Support Staff**
http://educationsupportstaff.co.uk/

The following is not meant to be an exhaustive list of reading, but rather suggestions to get you and your novice teachers started in the right direction:

★ **Building A Better Teacher by Elizabeth Green**
★ **A Framework for Understanding Poverty by Ruby Payne**
★ **Mindset by Carol Dweck**
★ **The One Minute Manager by Ken Blanchard and Spencer Johnson**
★ **Schools For All Kinds of Minds by Mary-Dean Barringer**
★ **The Courage to Teach by Parker J. Palmer**
★ **The First Days of School: How To Be An Effective Teacher by Harry Wong**

★ The 7 Habits of Highly Effective People by Stephen Covey

★ Teach Like a Champion by Doug Lemov

★ Teach Like a Pirate by Dave Burgess

★ Teacher and Child by Hiam Ginott

★ Teaching with Poverty in Mind by Eric Jensen

★ What Is It About Me You Can't Teach? An Instructional Guide for the Urban Educator by Eleanor René Rodriguez and James Bellanca

KEEP THE ENGINE RUNNING— FINAL THOUGHTS

"Behind every successful person, there is one elementary truth: somewhere, somehow, someone cared about their growth and development." –Dr. Beverly Kaye

"Students taught by an effective teacher score 50% higher than those students taught by an ineffective teacher." –Linda Darling-Hammond, The Brookings Institute

"If teachers and administrators value mentoring highly and take it seriously, mentoring will attract caring and committed teachers who recognize the complex and challenging nature of classroom teaching. It will attract teachers who demonstrate their hope and optimism for the future by their willingness to help a new teacher discover the same joys and satisfactions that they have found in their own career." –ASCD

A lot is experienced in this journey; the destination is to move the new teachers into self-sufficient educators ready to mentor the next generation. We want them to develop a capacity and competence to make their own informed decisions. With a smooth-running engine, students will thrive and teachers will have a rewarding teaching career for the long haul.

ACKNOWLEDGMENTS

This book is dedicated to our husbands and families, who were our key supporters as we developed our careers in education and blended our passion, experience, and expertise to create this publication. It is also dedicated to the educators, students, and new teachers along our path who inspired, taught, guided, encouraged, and affirmed us.

Special thanks to Julie Salley, our consummate mentor, who modeled best practices by providing cutting-edge professional development, encouraging us to reach our full capacity, and always taking time to "sharpen the saw." ("The 7 Habits of Highly Effective People" by Stephen Covey).

Thanks to Dr. Von Perot, who, as a new teacher coming from industry, taught us the power of allowing new teachers to find their own voice in their classrooms. Dr. Perot also provided her editing expertise and affirmed the need for administrators to be leaders in addressing the unique needs of novice teachers.

TAKE THE NEXT STEP

Research shows that formal mentoring programs for new and second-career teachers are seen as vital for teacher retention and academic student achievement.

This book will benefit those who are assigned, delegated or chosen to steer the challenge of mentoring novice teachers on their campus. This book is not intended to replace a formal new-teacher induction program, but rather to complement what may already be in place for new teachers in any district or corporation. Reading this book in its entirety chronologically or using it as a reference guide will move your mentoring practice forward.

The questions, ideas, and relevant information presented need to be considered, examined, and answered through the lens of individual districts, school beliefs, values, missions, and curricula.

Along our journey, administrators have requested a resource to better inform and support themselves, their instructional coaches, grade-level chairs and department chairs to enhance the first-year experience for novice teachers. This book is the answer and can be used in conjunction with an existing program or be your fundamental resource for supporting new teachers.

To order books (bulk pricing available) or receive additional support and information, please contact:

Cindy Daniels
602-525-1701
cdaniels369@gmail.com

Karen Martin
480-586-8743
kjrmartin41@gmail.com

Our best,

Cindy and Karen